Victoria Mary

George

THE HOUSE
OF WINDSOR

A ROYAL HISTORY OF ENGLAND

THE HOUSE
OF WINDSOR

BY ANDREW ROBERTS

EDITED BY
ANTONIA FRASER

University of California Press
Berkeley   Los Angeles

University of California Press
Berkeley and Los Angeles, California

Published by arrangement with Cassell & Co

The text of *The House of Windsor* is taken from the single-volume
The Lives of the Kings & Queens of England, first published in the United Kingdom
in 1975 by Weidenfeld & Nicolson, revised in 1993 and 1998.

Cataloging-in-Publication data is on file with the Library of Congress.

ISBN 0-520-22803-0

Jacket images: front © Camera Press (coronation portrait of Elizabeth II by Cecil Beaton);
back © Camera Press (the Annual Garter ceremony at Windsor Castle, June 1996).

Endpapers: Card commemorating the visit of the Prince and Princess of Wales, later George V
and Queen Mary, to India in 1905-6. *Page 2*: Portrait of Elizabeth II by Pietro Annigoni.

Printed and bound in Italy.
9 8 7 6 5 4 3 2 1

CONTENTS

INTRODUCTION

The House of Saxe-Coburg-Gotha became the House of Windsor on 17 July 1917. This unequivocally anti-German gesture was perfectly judged and well received by a nation viciously embroiled in the First World War. Windsor, after a minor title once held by Edward III, had been the suggestion of Lord Stamfordham, the Private Secretary of the reigning George V.

There is something of a contrast between the orderly popular image of King George V and the tumultuous course of his twenty-five year rule over Britain and her far-flung Empire. Prince George Frederick, the younger son of King Edward VII, might seem ill-equipped to preside over such a complex period. How was such an essentially ordinary, upright man to cope with the problems that beset the monarchy unremittingly from his accession in 1910 until his death in 1936? To a remarkable extent, King George V was in fact the right man in the right place, or at any rate occupying it, at the right time. His time in the navy had demanded discipline and common sense, tolerance and an ability to 'get along'. It turned out to be appropriate training for a man who reigned bravely and modestly at the moment when the British Empire reached its territorial zenith.

'After I am dead,' George V had predicted, 'the boy will ruin himself in twelve months' – the 'boy' was his son, Edward, Prince of Wales. Handsome, charming, vain and somewhat superficial (he found his studies at Oxford 'a dreadful chore'), it was above all Prince Edward's predilection for the 'wrong' woman that drew his father's temper. In 1934 Edward met Mrs Ernest Simpson (née Warfield), and began a genuine love affair that was to define the rest of his life. By November of 1936, a mere eleven months after Edward became King, it was clear that neither the establishment nor, as Prime Minister Stanley Baldwin was convinced, polite society would conscience the thought of a twice-divorced American sitting on the British throne. On 10 December 1936, King Edward VIII signed the Instrument of Abdication and on 12

December left for Austria. The stand-off between the Duke of Windsor, as he became, and the Palace began.

Two things are clear: that blame for the embittered relations that ensued should be shared and that the former King's life took on the air of both tragedy and farce. Having undertaken never again to live in the United Kingdom, the Duke and Duchess, the former having served for a time as the Governor of the Bahamas, retired to a beautiful house granted them by the City of Paris. Some glamour remained, but it was easily pricked. Shortly before the Duke of Windsor's death in 1972, Prince Charles wrote in his diary of a visit: 'The eye then wandered to a table in the hall on which lay a red box with "The King" on it.'

One of those who signed as witness to the Instrument of Abdication was Edward's brother Albert, Duke of York; and on 12 May 1937, the day that had been planned for Edward VIII's coronation, Albert was himself crowned George VI. Shy and lachrymose (he wrote that on the evening before the Abdication he 'broke down and sobbed like a child'), Albert grew up in the shadow of his father and elder brother, afflicted by ill health and a stammer; but if charisma was lacking, transparent decency was not. At his death on 6 February 1952, George VI was deeply and genuinely mourned as a monarch who had seen his country through the crisis of abdication and worked tirelessly and selflessly with his wife, the present Queen Mother, to ameliorate the devastation of the Second World War.

Only a week earlier George VI had waved his twenty-five-year-old daughter, Princess Elizabeth, and her husband, Prince Philip, off on a tour of the Empire; she returned prematurely and in mourning as Queen Elizabeth II. The coronation on 2 June 1952 was televized at the Queen's insistence and watched by twenty million Britons; it provoked little less than national rejoicing.

Much of the remainder of Elizabeth II's reign has been played out in front of a worldwide audience that has shown at times an almost pathological interest in her family. The personal difficulties of Elizabeth II's life do not need to be iterated here; what should be weighed against the nadir of the 'annus horribilis' are the genuine affection and gratitude of a nation that were occasioned by the Silver Jubilee in 1977. In a time of seemingly constant change, Elizabeth II has kept a promise of lifelong service and remains a symbol of stability and tradition; a fact that will surely be recognized at her Golden Jubilee in 2002.

THE HOUSE OF WINDSOR

1910-

GEORGE V 1910-36

EDWARD VIII 1936

GEORGE VI 1936-52

ELIZABETH II 1952-

Opposite: The Queen Mother, with her grandsons, Princes Harry and William, celebrating her ninety-ninth birthday in 1999.

THE HOUSES OF SAXE-COBURG-GOTHA and WINDSOR

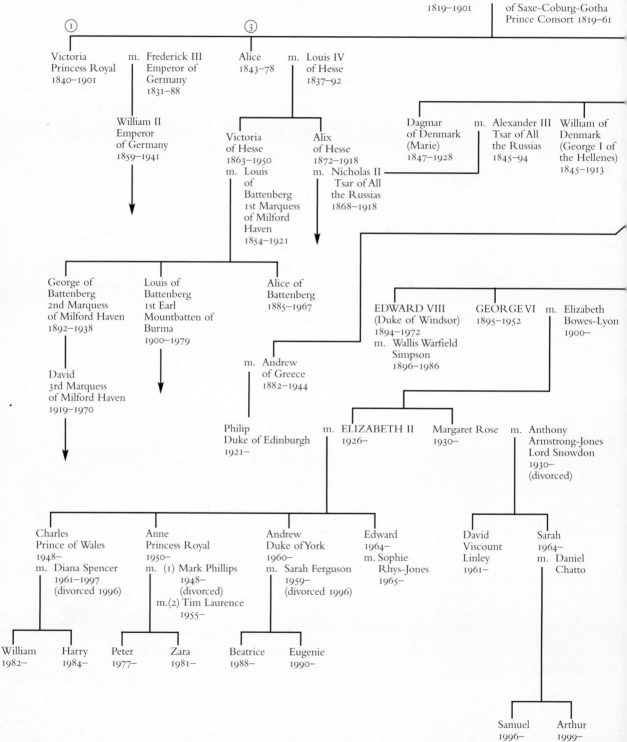

VICTORIA m. Albert
1819–1901 of Saxe-Coburg-Gotha
Prince Consort 1819–61

①

Victoria m. Frederick III
Princess Royal Emperor of
1840–1901 Germany
1831–88

William II
Emperor
of Germany
1859–1941

③

Alice m. Louis IV
1843–78 of Hesse
1837–92

Victoria
of Hesse
1863–1950
m. Louis
of
Battenberg
1st Marquess
of Milford
Haven
1854–1921

Alix
of Hesse
1872–1918
m. Nicholas II
Tsar of All
the Russias
1868–1918

Dagmar m. Alexander III William of
of Denmark Tsar of All Denmark
(Marie) the Russias (George I of
1847–1928 1845–94 the Hellenes)
1845–1913

George of
Battenberg
2nd Marquess
of Milford Haven
1892–1938

Louis of
Battenberg
1st Earl
Mountbatten of
Burma
1900–1979

Alice of
Battenberg
1885–1967

EDWARD VIII
(Duke of Windsor)
1894–1972
m. Wallis Warfield
Simpson
1896–1986

GEORGE VI m. Elizabeth
1895–1952 Bowes-Lyon
1900–

David
3rd Marquess
of Milford Haven
1919–1970

m. Andrew
of Greece
1882–1944

Philip
Duke of Edinburgh
1921–

m. ELIZABETH II
1926–

Margaret Rose m. Anthony
1930– Armstrong-Jones
Lord Snowdon
1930–
(divorced)

Charles
Prince of Wales
1948–
m. Diana Spencer
1961–1997
(divorced 1996)

Anne
Princess Royal
1950–
m. (1) Mark Phillips
1948–
(divorced)
m.(2) Tim Laurence
1955–

Andrew
Duke of York
1960–
m. Sarah Ferguson
1959–
(divorced 1996)

Edward
1964–
m. Sophie
Rhys-Jones
1965–

David
Viscount
Linley
1961–

Sarah
1964–
m. Daniel
Chatto

William Harry
1982– 1984–

Peter Zara
1977– 1981–

Beatrice Eugenie
1988– 1990–

Samuel Arthur
1996– 1999–

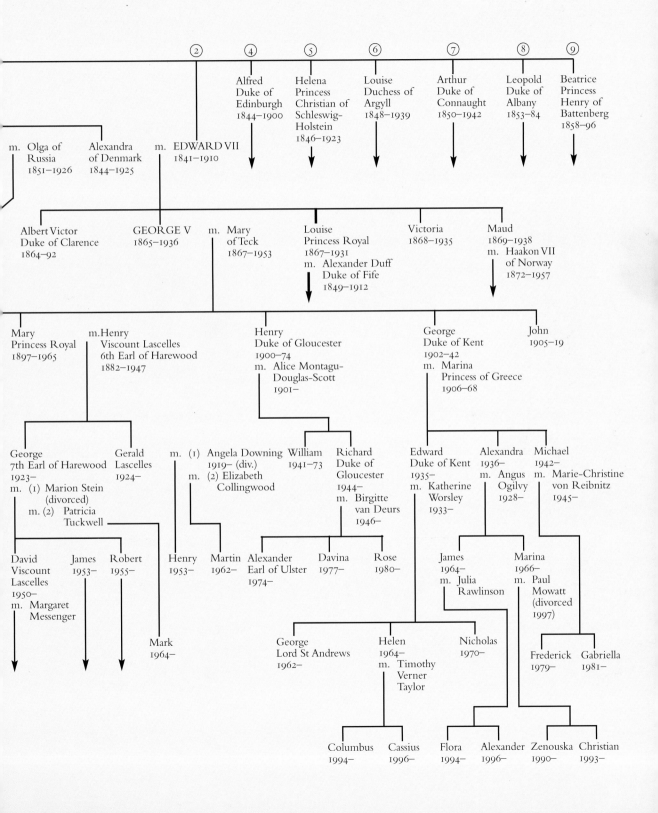

THE ROYAL ARMS

GEORGE IV AND WILLIAM IV SUCCEEDED to both the British and German possessions and so bore the post-1816 version of the arms unaltered.

On the death of William IV in 1837 the crowns were divided. That of Great Britain devolved upon his niece Victoria but that of Hanover, as it could not pass to a woman, went to the next male heir, William's brother Ernest Augustus, Duke of Cumberland.

Queen Victoria removed the shield and crown from the centre of the arms and was left with the royal arms as borne today by the present Queen. In the illustration are included three representations of the royal crown. That on the left was often used by Victoria although it is strictly speaking incorrect; that in the centre was also used by Victoria later in her reign whilst that on the right was used by George V and George VI.

The point to remember is that the shape of the crown is not significant, other than it reflects the artistic taste of the sovereign. What is important is that the crown in the arms is the royal crown, symbolising St Edward's crown, which is used at a coronation, itself symbolising the temporal authority and dominion of the sovereign under God.

It is sometimes remarked that now that the Queen is Queen of Canada, Australia and various other Commonwealth countries, the royal arms should symbolise this fact. Against doing this it must be argued that the constant comings and goings within the Commonwealth would necessitate endless alteration of the royal arms, which would be impracticable. The problem has been solved by there being separate arms for each of the Commonwealth kingdoms, in which the crown is the unifying factor.

The other question which is often raised is the apparent neglect of Wales, which has never featured in the royal arms. This is because Wales was never a separate kingdom, ruled by an English king. In 1302 it was absorbed into England but became a principality. Today Wales is represented armorially in the arms of the Prince of Wales. Over the royal arms he bears the old arms of the princes of North Wales, now used to represent the whole principality, ensigned by the coronet of the heir apparent.

GEORGE V *r.* 1910-36

O N 17 JULY 1917, THE PRIVY COUNCIL proclaimed that henceforth the royal family would be called the House of Windsor, having divested itself of its previous surname, as well as 'all other German degrees, styles, titles, dignatories, honours and appelations'. After a number of alternatives were considered – including Plantagenet, York, England, Lancaster, D'Este and Fitzroy – George V's Private Secretary Lord Stamfordham's suggestion of Windsor was adopted, after a minor title once held by Edward III.

This anti-German gesture, made at a critical juncture of the First World War, produced one of Kaiser William II's few jokes, when he remarked with heavy Teutonic humour that he looked forward to attending a performance of 'The Merry Wives of Saxe-Coburg-Gotha'. A more serious and altogether grander criticism came from the Bavarian Count Albrecht von Montgelas, who observed that 'the true royal tradition died on that day in 1917 when, for a mere war, King George V changed his name'. In fact the College of Arms could not even determine whether the royal surname had originally been Guelph, Wettin or Saxe-Coburg-Gotha in the first place.

The effect in Britain was instantaneous and overwhelmingly positive. With the whole family swapping Germanic-sounding for overtly British names – the Teck family became the Cambridges and took the earldom of Athlone, the Battenbergs were transformed into Mountbattens with the marquisate of Milford Haven – the royal family proclaimed itself thoroughly British, to national applause. Despite the whispering campaign against some members of his family that they were pro-German, King George V had always been quintessentially British, finding German

Opposite: King George V and Queen Mary in the summer 1914 edition of the *Illustrated London News.* Their marriage of mutual affection was one of the most successful modern royal unions.

Their Royal Highnesses
Prince Albert Victor, Duke
of Clarence (left), and Prince
George Frederick Ernest
Albert, later to become King
George V (right).

'a rotten language'. When H. G. Wells criticised 'an alien and uninspiring court', the King retorted, 'I may be uninspiring, but I'll be damned if I'm an alien.'

Born at Marlborough House on 3 June 1865, Prince George Frederick Ernest Albert was not expected to succeed to the throne, and had a happier, less pressured childhood as a result. His elder brother, Prince Albert Victor, Duke of Clarence – known as 'Eddy' – was a dissolute youth, who took after their father the future Edward VII in flouting the social and sexual mores of the day, in a way which the conscientious, dutiful and genuinely Christian young Prince George never did. In a dynasty long plagued by bad parent–child relationships, however, Prince George's love of and utter devotion to his father – which was fully reciprocated – was a refreshing exception to the rule.

The greatest influence on the Prince's personality was not, however, his uniformly happy childhood, so much as his fifteen years of hardy service in the Royal Navy. Joining HMS *Britannia* as a naval cadet in 1877, Prince George soon showed genuine accomplishments in a profession which was watching closely for the smallest sign of nepotism. He became Britain's most widely-travelled king, serving in the West Indies, South America, Australia, Japan, South Africa and China in various vessels, sometimes experiencing serious danger.

This period aboard ship gave him a disciplined, ultra-conservative outlook, a bluff manner, a certain saltiness of language, a commonsensical attitude and a profound belief in the ideals of the British Empire, all of which were to stay with him throughout his life. In 1885, by then promoted to first lieutenant after a period on the North America station in the corvette HMS *Canada*, Prince George won a first class in seamanship, gunnery and torpedos from the Royal Naval College at Greenwich, a justifiable source of pride to him. Afterwards he served for three years on the Mediterranean station before acquiring his own command, of the gunboat HMS *Thrush* in 1890.

It was whilst as a commander, on illness furlough, that he heard of the death from pneumonia of his elder brother on 14 January 1892. This meant a complete alteration of every aspect of his existence, from being a well-connected officer destined for future well-earned naval commands, to being heir apparent to the heir apparent to the throne of the largest empire the world had ever seen. His nautical career over, he was created Duke of York and given residences in York House in St James's Palace as well as York Cottage near Sandringham House.

Engagement photograph taken at Luton Hoo on 5 December 1892 of the Duke of Clarence and Princess Victoria Mary of Teck. The Duke died little over a month later and Victoria Mary later married his younger brother George.

George and Mary on their wedding day, 6 July 1893. A genuine love match, this royal marriage was one of the most successful of 'modern' times.

A few weeks before his very premature death at twenty-six, his brother had got engaged to Princess Victoria Mary of Teck, known in the family as May. Rather than allow this demure, sensible and bright girl out of the family, Queen Victoria acted decisively to arrange that the Duke of York carry on the suit. Thus a country which was at that time obsessed with the proprieties of men marrying their deceased wife's sister, on 6 July 1893 enthusiastically celebrated the Duke of York's marriage to his deceased brother's fiancée.

The wedding took place in St James's Chapel, attended by the crowned and soon-to-be crowned heads of Europe, including Queen Victoria, the King of Denmark and the Tsarevich of Russia, the future Nicholas II. It turned out to be one of the most successful royal marriages of modern times, a genuine love match in which Princess, later Queen, Mary's qualities complemented her husband's and provided him with a source of sound advice distinct from that proffered by politicians and courtiers. Queen Mary proved the personification of royal rectitude, an impossibly grand, even terrifying figure who yet also provided genuine domestic tranquillity for her husband, and rescued the popular conception of royal family life from its louche Edwardian image.

Children followed with impressive rapidity and regularity. Prince Edward (later King Edward VIII) was born in 1894, Prince Albert (later King George VI) in 1895, Princess Mary in 1897, Prince Henry (later Duke of Gloucester) in 1900, Prince George (later Duke of Kent) in 1902 and Prince John (an epileptic who died aged only thirteen) in 1905. Although in his memoirs the Duke of Windsor was keen to present his parents as stern, somewhat heartless disciplinarians – a myth that has endured to this day and has been greatly exaggerated in the retelling – the King and Queen should be judged by the exacting standards of the Victorian upper classes rather than by today's more indulgent child-rearing mores. The problems they had with the wayward Prince

Edward were largely his own fault, and his accusations of parental harshness can usually be traced back to the Duke of Windsor's attempts to excuse his subsequent behaviour.

On the death of Queen Victoria on 22 January 1901, and the accession of his father as Edward VII, the Duke of York became Duke of Cornwall as well, and took a major step towards the throne of the King–Emperor. He got closer to the King in a physical sense also, as his desk was moved beside his father's at Buckingham Palace so they could work side by side whenever they were in London. Unlike his mother Queen Victoria, who had deliberately kept her heir starved of official papers, Edward VII ensured that his son saw all important state documents.

King George V and Queen Mary with their six children. This photograph was taken in 1905 or 1906 and shows Mary holding Price John, an epileptic who died at the age of thirteen.

Opposite: George v, 'the Sailor King', is featured on a magazine cover at the helm of his famous yacht *Britannia.* His abiding love of the sea dated from his time in the Royal Navy as a young man.

To help him with them, the Duke – who in November 1901 became Prince of Wales – inherited Sir Arthur Bigge, later Lord Stamfordham, as his Private Secretary from Queen Victoria. This counsellor, suffused in wisdom and experience, was also to become a trusted friend until his death, still in the job, in 1931.

In the nine years of the Edwardian era, the Prince of Wales enjoyed himself to the full, but was always heavily conscious of the burden which would eventually fall on him. Although a competition-standard golfer and tennis player, it was in yachting and shooting that he really excelled. One of the finest half-dozen shots in the country, he and six other guns once bagged 10,000 birds in four days at Sandringham. A keen yachtsman, he won racing cups at Cowes and established his right to be nicknamed 'the Sailor King' alongside William IV. More sedentary was his passion for stamp-collecting, where he built up the world's greatest collection – over 250,000 specimens housed in 325 big volumes. In his near-obsessional interest in uniforms and decorations he followed the family tradition, but he could also be sartorially innovative – the creases in his trousers were found at the sides, for example, and he pulled his tie through a ring rather than knotting it.

The most important aspect of his time as Prince of Wales and his father's understudy, during which he dutifully attended many House of Lords debates, was his commitment to the Empire; he believed in it implicitly as the foremost global agency for promoting peace and human progress. On their 231-day tour of Australia, New Zealand and Canada in 1901, he and the Princess travelled 45,000 miles, received 544 addresses, laid a score of foundation stones and shook hands with no less than 24,855 people. On his return he delivered a widely reported speech at the Guildhall on 5 December 1901, in which he said that 'the Old Country must wake up if she intends to maintain her old position of pre-eminence in her Colonial trade against foreign competitors'.

'At 11.45 beloved Papa passed peacefully away', the new King-Emperor

George v rides behind the body of his father at the King's funeral in 1910. He is flanked by, on the left, his cousin Kaiser Wilhelm of Germany and, on the right, his uncle the Duke of Connaught.

H.M. THE KING   AS A YACHTSMAN

King George V with David Lloyd George, who persuaded the King to abstain from alcohol for the duration of the Great War and set an example to munition workers. In between the two men is their host, the Mackintosh of Mackintosh.

George V wrote in his diary on 6 May 1910, 'and I have lost my best friend and the best of fathers.' The moment he had been both dreading and preparing for over the seventeen years since his brother's death had come. The mantle of imperial responsibility had fallen upon a Norfolk squire of nearly forty-five, with deeply conservative views, few intellectual or artistic interests, little oratorical ability, but a passionate desire to do his duty.

The pre-Great War era, now often seen as a tranquil, even lazy period of cucumber sandwiches and croquet on well-cut lawns, was in fact an extremely uncertain and worrying time for those concerned with defending the social order. Forces such as organised labour, Irish republicanism, Indian nationalism, foreign protectionism, militant suffragettes and anarchist revolutionaries – let alone the High Seas Fleet of the Imperial German Navy – now seemed to threaten British policy-makers in a way their nineteenth-century parents and grandparents hardly contemplated. The period between George V's accession in May 1910 and the outbreak of the Great War in August four years later saw a succession of crises which the King generally tried to avert by conciliation and appeasement.

The reign started off on this note when on 16 November 1910 the Liberal prime minister Herbert Asquith and his Leader of the House of Lords the Marquis of Crewe extracted a secret 'hypothetical understanding' from George V that in the event of the Liberals winning the forthcoming general election – the second that year – the King would sanction the creation of possibly hundreds of new Liberal peers, enough to defeat dogged Unionist resistance and pass a Parliament Bill restricting the powers of the House of Lords. The Parliamentary guerrilla warfare had been going on since the Unionist peers had flung out Lloyd George's 'People's' Budget the previous year. The ultra-Tory Stamfordham advised resistance to Asquith's demands; this would have placed the King in the highly invidious position of appearing to support the Unionists in an election, but his master cleaved instead to the view of his other private secretary, his father's former adviser the more Liberal-minded Lord Knollys, who counselled surrender to the duly constituted government's demands.

By making public, in a debate on 10 August 1911, the agreement the King had regarded as secret, the Liberal government managed to browbeat the Unionists into surrender. It took the King a long time to forgive Asquith; twenty-one years later he told Lord Crewe that he regarded 'forcing my hand' as sheer bullying of a fledgling monarch, 'the dirtiest thing ever done … a dirty, low-down trick'. It was the implication in asking for a formal promise that he could not be trusted to do the right thing should the constitutional moment arise that the King most resented, and it served to confirm his generally low view of politicians.

Politics took a back seat in the great coronation celebrations of 22 June 1911. These were accompanied by the magnificent Spithead Review, in which the King proudly sailed around the greatest fleet ever assembled in human history. He then travelled to Delhi where at a huge Durbar he presented himself as King-Emperor to the teeming

George V presents himself as King-Emperor to his Indian dominions, Delhi 12 December 1911. George was a firm supporter of the British Empire believing that it was the foremost global agency for promoting peace and human progress.

'Coronation Lunch for King
George V and Queen Mary',
by Solomon Joseph Solomon.

Opposite: Coronation portrait
of King George V and
Queen Mary. After the death
of his brother, George spent
seventeen years dreading
and preparing for his ascent
to the throne.

millions in the newly declared capital of the greatest of his dominions
and took the oaths of allegiance from all the Indian princes.

On his return he found a smouldering situation in Ireland, where
the Ulster Unionists were resolving to repudiate the Irish Home Rule
Bill, by force if necessary. After the Bill was thrown out by the House
of Lords, and Ulstermen began armed drilling in public, the King made
serious behind-the-scenes efforts to resolve the situation peacefully.
The senior figures on all sides were invited to a round table conference
at Buckingham Palace in July 1914, where they failed to agree, and
anyhow soon found that events on the continent were overshadowing
their deliberations.

For on 4 August 1914 the First World War broke out, and the King
faced the greatest challenge of any monarch since George III had
presided over the Seven Years' War a century and a half previously. 'I
cannot share your hardships,' the King told the troops in the trenches,
'but my heart is with you every hour of the day.' In the course of the
conflict the King made numerous morale-boosting visits to the Fleet
and Army, field hospitals, factories and almost every other part of the

Second Army Headquarters in Blendecques: George V awards Second Lieutenant Knox with the Victoria Cross on 5 August 1918.

Following pages: George V visiting troops at the front during the First World War.

Opposite: The King encourages a young war worker in Sunderland, on one of his many tours to boost morale during the war.

war effort. He distributed over 58,000 decorations. He supported Earl Haig against Lloyd George, on the grounds that the soldier on the spot probably understood the situation better than the man in Whitehall, with results which are still subject to historical debate today, albeit one which increasingly seems to be going Haig and George V's way. In October 1915 he broke his pelvis falling from a horse whilst on an inspection of the Royal Flying Corps on the Western Front, which, once misdiagnosed, gave him great pain.

The King and Queen Mary abjured alcohol for the duration of the war, in a largely vain attempt to set an example to the munition workers. It was Lloyd George's idea, and one the King was understandably reluctant about and found 'a great bore'. Nevertheless it helped to dispel the unpleasant but persistent rumour that he was an alcoholic. (Similarly a myth that he was a bigamist who had contracted a marriage with an admiral's daughter whilst on service in Malta had been scotched in 1911 when a newspaper editor, E. F. Mylius, was imprisoned for twelve months for criminal libel.)

Photograph taken in Berlin during 1913 of King George v and his cousin Tsar Nicholas ii. In March 1917 George feared unrest if Nicholas were granted political asylum it Britain.

Only on one occasion during the war did the royal nerve break, when as a result of a ludicrously overblown fear of domestic republicanism – at a time when millions were under arms fighting for King and country – George v countermanded Lloyd George's March 1917 attempt to give his deposed cousin Tsar Nicholas ii political asylum in Britain. Fearing that it might inflame a socialist and republican outcry amongst the industrial working classes should he send a British battleship to bring over the Tsar, the King effectively condemned 'cousin Nicky' to remain in Russia, with consequences few could have foreseen at the time, months before the Bolshevik revolution.

Rarely smiling – 'Sailors on duty don't smile' – but giving an admired national lead, the King never attempted to grab the limelight from politicians during the war, still less from the Services. The British people seemed to sense this, and when the day of victory finally came on 11 November 1918 – 'the greatest in the history of the country', wrote the King in his diary – it was to Buckingham Palace that they flocked to celebrate all night, the royal family waving from the balcony of the façade which he had had refaced in 1912. With peace came an end to his love of travel. In the eighteen years left of his reign he only went abroad for eight weeks, of which five were spent convalescing on a Mediterranean cruise.

The collapse of the Russian, Austrian, German and Ottoman empires left the British monarchy looking exposed as an institution, and all the King's political efforts were henceforth devoted to appeasing those dangerous new forces which he perceived might threaten the British constitutional settlement in the future. In his dealings, therefore, with the Labour Party, trade unions, Mahatma Gandhi, Irish republicans and eventually even the continental fascist movements, his first instinct was to try to conciliate and find some common, middle ground. In 1921 he played an important role in encouraging the Lloyd George coalition government to be as generous as possible to Eamon de Valera during the foundation of the Irish Free State. He wanted every possible effort made to ensure that the new self-governing southern Irish state should be born with as little bitterness as possible.

In 1923, advised and abetted by Lord Stamfordham, he chose the relatively junior Stanley Baldwin to succeed Bonar Law as prime minister, instead of the vastly better qualified former Viceroy and Foreign Secretary Lord Curzon. They felt that it would be insulting to the Labour Party not to have a prime minister in the House of Commons, able to answer questions there. When Labour came to power the following January, the King, for all his private distrust of socialism, observed minutely all the constitutional niceties and gradually came to admire the first Labour prime minister, Ramsay MacDonald. 'Today twenty-three years ago Grandmama died,' he wrote in his diary the day before MacDonald formed the first Labour government, 'I wonder what she would have thought.' It is not hard to guess, considering that Queen Victoria even regarded the Gladstonian Liberals as dangerous radicals.

Silver Jubilee Thanksgiving service for King George V in 1935. Commenting typically on the service, he said that there had been 'too many damned parsons getting in the way'.

When the General Strike broke out in 1926, the King called for an end to bitterness. This sort of well-meaning message to the nation reached far further when in 1932 the King made the first of his Christmas broadcasts to the Empire. These simple, homely, Christian if somewhat saccharine addresses, through the powerful new medium of radio, helped connect the monarchy with the people more personally than had ever been previously possible.

By then the King's personal authority was unassailable, his reign universally considered a success; indeed the institution of monarchy in Britain saw something of a golden age between 1918 and the King's death in 1936. For all his distaste of 'advertisement' he had a fine sense of what today is called public relations. When the economic crisis known as the Great Depression threatened sterling in 1931 he voluntarily surrendered a significant part of his Civil List to the Exchequer, and called a conference of party leaders that eventually led to the formation of a National Government by Ramsay MacDonald and Stanley Baldwin.

'You have kept up the dignity of the office,' he admiringly wrote to an ill MacDonald who was considering retirement in June 1934, 'without using it to give you dignity.' The resignation of Sir Samuel Hoare in December 1935, over the notorious Hoare–Laval Pact that had been negotiated in Paris, produced a classically George v joke, when he said to the departing minister: 'You know what they're all saying, no more coals to Newcastle, no more Hoares to Paris.' He later complained to Hoare's successor Anthony Eden, 'The fellow didn't even laugh.'

The Silver Jubilee celebrations in 1935 saw a huge national outpouring of thanks and affection to the King and Queen, although typically the King thought of the church service that there had been 'too many damned parsons getting in the way'. Through twenty-five years of international and domestic upheavals the King had, to use a nautical metaphor he might have appreciated, steered a steady course. The fact that his natural reaction to crises was always to call a conference and hope the goodwill of the participants would help find

The 1935 Silver Jubilee celebrations: the royal family at Buckingham Palace (above); Milcote Street in London (below); and a commemorative postcard (opposite).

agreement cannot be held against a monarch who saw his political task largely in terms of effecting conciliation.

The last great worry for the King, the personification of that generation of Britons who, in John Betjeman's words, were 'old men who never cheated, never doubted', was over the conduct of his eldest son Edward, the Prince of Wales. This intensely self-disciplined, blue-eyed churchman, a stickler for form who read the Bible daily, was disgusted to hear of his heir carrying on with an American divorcee, two of whose husbands were still living. He predicted disaster for the coming reign, when his own loud voice, common sense and explosive temper could no longer affect his son's activities. 'After I am dead', he predicted dolefully, 'the boy will ruin himself in twelve months'. In fact it took only eleven.

Another disaster he foresaw was the Second World War. His experience of its predecessor made him almost a pacifist when contemplating the possibility of another Anglo-German conflict. 'I will not have another war,' he told Lloyd George in May 1935, 'I will not. The last one was none of my doing and if there is another one and we are threatened with being brought into it, I will go to Trafalgar Square myself and wave a red flag myself rather than allow this country to be brought in.'

SILVER JUBILEE

To Commemorate
the Twenty-fifth
Anniversary of
the Accession of
KING GEORGE
THE FIFTH
to the Throne

May 6th 1910
May 6th 1935

Service of Thanksgiving,
St. Paul's Cathedral,
London.

8597.

A newspaper seller conveys the news of the death of George V. One of the greatest monarchs, and much loved, he died on 20 January 1936.

Opposite: King George V lying in state in Westminster Hall on 23 January 1936. Gentlemen at Arms and Yeoman of the Guard watch over the coffin, which is draped with the Royal Standard and bears the symbols of Regal power: the crown, orb and sceptre.

On 20 January 1936 one of the greatest British monarchs died, after a short illness. His reputation for salty, down-to-earth language created a myth that his last words were 'Bugger Bognor', after a doctor had ingratiatingly suggested that he might recuperate in the same seaside resort as he had after a serious illness in 1929. In fact the story probably dates from the King's response to the town's request to be styled Bognor Regis for its part in the royal recovery, which Stamfordham took as approval. In 1936 though, the King's actual last words were far more characteristic. A Privy Council had somewhat officiously been forced upon him as he lay on his deathbed, in order to organize arrangements should he become incapacitated. 'Gentlemen,' he told them when he felt capable of speaking, 'I am so sorry for keeping you waiting like that. I am unable to concentrate.' So he died as he had lived, bravely and modestly doing to his duty without undue regard for self.

EDWARD VIII *r.* 1936

*A*T LONG LAST I AM ABLE TO SAY a few words of my own' said Edward VIII in a radio broadcast the day after his abdication in 1936. 'You must believe me when I tell you that I have found it impossible to carry the heavy burden of responsibility and to discharge my duties as King as I would wish to do without the help and support of the woman I love.'

At the time the Abdication seemed almost a defining moment, but in the light of international events three years later it has been relegated to a footnote of the history of the 1930s, albeit a fascinating one. The short reign of the charismatic but incurably vain and lightweight King still has the capacity to divide opinion between those who consider old-fashioned values and duty to be the paramount considerations for monarchy, and those who believe love and being true to the dictates of the heart matter more.

Prince Edward Albert Christian George Andrew Patrick was born on 23 June 1894, the eldest son of the Duke of York (later King George v) and Princess (later Queen) Mary. In the confusing Windsor tradition of rarely calling people by their real names he was nicknamed 'David'. Queen Victoria doted on him; it was the first time in history that four generations of monarchy lived contemporaneously.

Although he later attempted to convince himself and others otherwise, he had a relatively happy childhood, and there is a mass of evidence, not least his own correspondence, testifying to the varied activities and contented nature of his upbringing. Like his father and younger brother Bertie (later George VI) he entered the Navy young, joining the Royal Naval College, Dartmouth, in May 1909. His disastrous showing in the exams there might have been the fault of his tutor

Opposite: Sir Edward Munnings's portrait of Edward, Prince of Wales. The handsome and charming Prince was everywhere adulated, and many looked forward to his reign as an era of youth and optimism.

The investiture of Edward, Prince of Wales, at Caernavon Castle in July 1911. He took the trouble to learn a few words of Welsh from Lloyd George to recite at the ceremony.

teaching the wrong syllabus, but even when years later he went up to Oxford the head of his college began a report with the words: 'Bookish he will never be'.

In May 1910 his grandfather Edward VII died and Prince Edward became heir to the throne. The blond young Prince made a tremendous impression in 1911 at the coronation service, when in his Garter robes he vowed allegiance to his father. Similarly, everyone admired the way in which at his investiture as Prince of Wales at Caernarvon Castle later that year he recited the few words of Welsh which Lloyd George had taught him.

But already he was beginning to speak his own mind, a course of action which was to lead to ever more severe clashes with his father. Complaining about the 'preposterous rig' he had to wear at the investiture, he gave notice to the court of a temperament which was over the following quarter-century to irritate and finally infuriate his parents and long-suffering courtiers.

In 1912 he went to France for four months to brush up on his French, but it was after that in Germany that he found a country he could fully admire, eventually becoming fluent in German while staying with royal cousins such as the King of Württemberg. He then passed his eight terms at Magdalen College, Oxford, in learning how to hunt, shoot, give and attend parties, drink and womanise, indeed enjoying all the traditional pursuits of the undergraduate barring the intellectual. Those he found 'a dreadful chore'.

In June 1914 he left Oxford for attachment to the Grenadier Guards, and when in August the Great War broke out he believed that at last he would have an opportunity to prove to his contemporaries that he had martial qualities. Writing to the Secretary of State for War Lord Kitchener, he explained how much he wished to go to the front line and serve in his regiment, and that because he had four brothers it hardly mattered drastically if he were killed there. Kitchener laconically answered, saying that his death would indeed cause few problems, but his capture might and that he was therefore to be relegated to a staff post behind the lines. Not so far behind as to be entirely out of danger, however, as on one visit to the front he left his car only minutes before a shell landed on it and killed his driver.

These vicarious threats to his safety were not enough to satisfy his sense of honour, and it was with acute disgust that he learned he had been awarded the Military Cross, knowing how others of his generation had had to distinguish themselves in action for it. It is not too fanciful to suggest that for the whole of the rest of his life he despised himself for not having undergone the hardships of his contemporaries in the trenches. This gnawing guilt was a common enough affliction in the post-war period, suffered even by people who had served but somehow survived. Prince Edward had a better excuse than most, as every attempt he made to go on active service had been blocked by the authorities, which ultimately meant his father.

After the war, George V unconsciously did everything possible to accentuate his son's feeling of inadequacy, even forbidding him to steeplechase after he sustained a particularly bad fall. Instead his good looks, sense of informality, supposed social conscience and undeniable charisma – part matinée idol, part international 'celebrity' of a royal type not really seen again until Diana, Princess of Wales – was harnessed to the cause of Empire. Long, well-organised and sensationally successful tours of Canada, America, New Zealand and Australia in 1919 and 1920 established the Prince's status as one of the world's great crowd-pleasers, and only Gandhi's political boycott partially spoiled what would have been another success in India. Ticker-tape welcomes in America, his courage during a railway accident in Australia, boyish high jinks on board ship with Lord Louis Mountbatten – all served to add to his reputation as an iconic royal figure with the common touch. He also tried to identify himself with the cause of ex-servicemen and the unemployed in the 1920s, which added greatly to his popularity at relatively little effort.

Clashes with the King multiplied as the stories of his exasperating and absurd whims, for which he would change long-standing arrangements and alter tight schedules at the last minute, percolated back to court. The tinder over which these rows could ignite might be as trivial as the Prince's trouser turnups, or a particularly informal photograph in a magazine. But the underlying concern was over his lack of a stable love-life, something the King and Queen worried about as he approached his fortieth year with only mistresses and no suitable consort in sight. The King, in contrast to the trust he had enjoyed from his own father, excluded the Prince of Wales from any real role of responsibility, which was almost an invitation to the Prince to behave irresponsibly instead.

Part of the reason why secret information was not generally included in the Prince's briefings was the Foreign Office's fear that he was a Nazi sympathiser – a situation which continued throughout his reign. His pro-German sentiments merged with a growing contempt for Parliamentary government and old-fashioned constitutional methods and gradually led him further than any other British royal in the direction of admiration for the fascist regimes in Germany and Italy. The sporty, unintelligent, fashionable, 'fast' set into which he moved in the early 1930s was peculiarly vulnerable to pro-fascist sentiment, and at least two of his close friends were 'ardent Hitlerites'.

By June 1933 Kaiser Wilhelm II's grandson Prince Louis Frederick was reporting that the Prince of Wales was 'quite pro-Hitler, and said it was no business of ours to interfere in Germany's internal affairs either re Jews or anything else and we might want one in England before long'. Two years later, in June 1935, the Prince had to be rebuked by his father for the warmth of his public declaration of friendship with Germany in a speech to ex-servicemen.

It was, however, sexual shenanigans, not political extremism, which worried the Palace most, just at the time when George V's failing health meant that they could do little about either. After enjoying the favours of Freda Dudley Ward, the wife of a Liberal MP, for nearly twenty years, he fell in love with a married American divorcee, Mrs Ernest Simpson (née Warfield), in 1934. Unlike earlier encounters with married, separated or divorced women – including Lady Furness with whom he went on safari, along with Lord Furness – this turned out to be more than merely sexual, but a genuine love affair. It was, as a marriage, to last for thirty-six years, longer indeed than most modern royal marriages. There is still speculation about the exact physical nature of the relationship, but it is certain that the Duchess was incapable of having children, a fact crucially not known to the royal family at the time.

Becoming King Edward VIII on 20 January 1936, his first act was to order that the Sandringham clocks which ran half an hour fast for reasons connected with his father's shooting passion, should be returned to the correct time. It was ironic that a moderniser should begin by turning the clocks back, and his two other modernising acts – substituting morning dress for court frock coats and occasionally walking short distances in public rather than always using a car – were equally easy and insubstantial.

Living at Fort Belvedere, a mock castle he had bought near Sunningdale in Berkshire in 1929, he continued his carefree Prince of Wales existence, failing to deal with his red boxes efficiently or punctually and sacking his father's retainers with the minimum of thanks and compensation for lifetimes of service. Far from the refreshing post-Victorian unstuffiness hailed by much of society, the new reign in fact heralded an undisciplined, excitable, lackadaisical future, for those who were close enough to know the truth about the King's real nature.

His only significant, and to the government potentially embarrassing act as King was taken on 18 November 1936 when, in greatcoat and bowler hat, the King toured the derelict Dowlais iron and steel works and met people who had been laid off there. 'These works brought all these people here', he declared. 'Something should be done to get them at work again.' It is a measure of his irresponsibility that he raised hopes in the hearts of the unemployed of South Wales only two days after he had intimated to Stanley Baldwin that he would abdicate sooner than lose Mrs Simpson. He knew perfectly well when he was raising the issue that he would probably not himself be around to see it through, but that

Baldwin's National Government would have to deal with the heightened but doomed expectations he left behind.

For on 16 November 1936 he calmly informed Baldwin that he was 'prepared to go'. The negotiations had gone on since 20 October 1936, when he had refused Baldwin's request to ask Mrs Simpson to withdraw the divorce petition which she had instituted. The following week a decree nisi was granted on the grounds that her husband, an American businessman and former Coldstream Guards Officer, had committed adultery, albeit in a pro forma way known in those days as 'hotel' adultery, a charade organised entirely for legal reasons. The decree was due to be made absolute in April 1937.

Rumours had been circulating in society ever since the King met Mrs Simpson in 1934, but especially since they went on a cruise down the Dalmatian coast together in the summer of 1936 on the yacht *Nahlin*. A self-denying ordinance on the part of the British press meant

A demonstrator in Downing Street at the height of the abdication crisis.

that the public were largely kept ignorant of what was happening, although rumours and foreign newspapers and magazines tended to filter through. As early as February 1936, the Labour politician J. H. Thomas told Harold Nicolson that the British people "ate 'aving no family life at court' and as a result 'it won't do, 'arold, I tell you that straight'. He was soon proved right.

On 1 December 1936 the Bishop of Bradford, the ideally named Dr Blunt, speaking at his diocesan conference about the forthcoming coronation, said of His Majesty's sense of duty that 'Some of us wish that he gave more positive signs of his awareness'. First the provincial press and then *The Times* used this outburst – to the Bishop's professed surprise – as the excuse to break their long, embarrassing, self-imposed restraint. But by the time the public en masse discovered what had been happening, the general outlines of the Abdication settlement had been laid. It is hard in those pre-opinion polling days to be certain of the public response to the news, but the responses to Conservative MPs from their constituency association chairmen convinced Baldwin that most respectable people rebelled at the thought of a twice-divorced American adventuress sitting on the British throne.

On 25 November the King brought up the possibility of marrying Mrs Simpson morganatically, a continental practice whereby she would be his legal wife, but not his official consort. After Baldwin had consulted the Cabinet – whose deliberations on the subject are still kept secret sixty-two years later – as well as the Labour Opposition and the prime ministers of the major dominions, he informed the King on 2 December that it was impracticable. Had the King attempted to stir up political trouble for the government – fascists and communists were

INSTRUMENT OF ABDICATION

I, Edward the Eighth, of Great Britain, Ireland, and the British Dominions beyond the Seas, King, Emperor of India, do hereby declare My irrevocable determination to renounce the Throne for Myself and for My descendants, and My desire that effect should be given to this Instrument of Abdication immediately.

In token whereof I have hereunto set My hand this tenth day of December, nineteen hundred and thirty six, in the presence of the witnesses whose signatures are subscribed.

SIGNED AT FORT BELVEDERE IN THE PRESENCE OF

The Instrument of Abdication, photographed at 10 Downing Street, with which Edward VIII relinquished the throne. It bears the signatures of Edward and his three brothers, Albert (later George VI), Henry, Duke of Gloucester, and George, Duke of Kent.

declaring their support for him, and both Lord Beaverbrook and Winston Churchill saw it as an opportunity for discomfiting Baldwin – he might have at least partially succeeded, but instead he soberly and responsibly decided to go quietly. Mrs Simpson, too, acted well during the crisis – offering to leave him if it would help him put his duty to the country before his love for her.

On 10 December 1936, the day after the Cabinet pleaded with him in vain to reconsider, King Edward VIII signed the Instrument of Abdication in the presence of his brothers at Fort Belvedere. The next day Parliament passed the Bill of Abdication which, when at 1.52 a.m. it received Royal Assent, ended his reign. That evening he broadcast to the people a message partly penned by Churchill, in which he stated that 'if at any time in the future I can be found of service to His Majesty in a private station I shall not fail'. But the Palace had other ideas, and fearful of his continuing popularity, far greater until the war than his younger brother the King's, they determined ruthlessly to sideline the ex-King for the rest of his life.

The Prince left for Austria in the early hours of 12 December 1936, to stay with Baron Eugene de Rothschild at Schloss Enzesfeld. He could not see Wallis Simpson, who was staying in the South of France, until her decree nisi had been made absolute. Soon after leaving England, the slights, rows and disagreements between the Duke of Windsor – as he was gazetted in March 1937 – and the British establishment began, which embittered relations for the rest of his life. As in any family row, all the blame cannot be attributed to one side or the other, but if the Windsors did react over-sensitively to events, that was because their wounds were kept deliberately raw.

First the new King, Edward's younger brother George VI, told Walter Monckton, the Duke's confidant and lawyer, that he no longer wished to receive the ex-King's telephone calls. Then the financial settlement, which had been arranged at a long formal meeting on the day of the signing of the Abdication, was reduced and reneged upon in tangible and humiliating ways, including the demand that in order to receive it the Duke had to undertake never to live in the United Kingdom. Then, after Mrs Simpson's divorce became absolute in April 1937 and the couple were reunited at Château de Condé in May, the news arrived that none of the royal family would attend the wedding. The fact that Lord Louis Mountbatten, who had been so keen to befriend the Duke all his life and who had agreed to be his best man

Opposite: A typical headline of Friday 11 December 1936 announcing Edward VIII's decision to abdicate.

Daily Herald

No. 6498   FRIDAY, DECEMBER 11, 1936   ONE PENNY

THE KING ABDICATES: WILL BROADCAST TO-NIGHT

LEAVING COUNTRY: MAY GO TO ROME

Duke Of York Succeeds To The Throne • Will Be Known As King George the Sixth

NEW RULER VISITS MOTHER

KING EDWARD VIII ABDICATED YESTERDAY. HE WILL BROADCAST TO THE NATION TO-NIGHT— "AS A PRIVATE INDIVIDUAL, OWING ALLEGIANCE TO THE NEW KING."

The broadcast will, it is expected, be made at 10 p.m., probably from Fort Belvedere. But there is a suggestion that it may be made from abroad, for it is known that the King wishes to leave the country at once.

It was stated last night that he might go to Rome—possibly by plane.

The new King is the Duke of York, who will almost certainly take the title of King George VI. Ten-year-old Princess Elizabeth becomes next in the line of succession.

Relinquishes

All His Titles

King Edward's last act as Monarch will be to sign a commission enabling the Royal Assent to be given to the Abdication Law which Parliament is rushing through all its stages to-day.

With the renunciation of the Throne the King relinquishes all his titles except that of Prince Edward, but it was rumoured last night that he might prefer to be known as plain " Mr. Windsor."

The new reign will be formally inaugurated by a Grand Accession Privy Council at Buckingham Palace to-night, and the new Monarch will be proclaimed, with all the heraldic pageantry of old, to-morrow.

Later in the day, both Houses of Parliament will meet so that M.P.s and Peers can take the oath of allegiance to the new King. The sitting is expected to last late into the evening.

Coronation Day, fixed for May 12, may not be postponed. Even if it is, the delay will be for only a few weeks.

" I Am Going to Marry Mrs. Simpson "

Mr. Baldwin made the dramatic announcement of King Edward's abdication in a hushed House of Commons yesterday afternoon, and explained how the King had told him, three weeks ago:—

"I AM GOING TO MARRY MRS. SIMPSON, AND I AM PREPARED TO GO."

It is significant that the Abdication Bill, by subsection 3 of Clause I, specially exempts the King from the operation of the Royal Marriages Act, so that he will be left as free as any ordinary citizen to marry whom he pleases.

The Abdication Paper was signed at Fort Belvedere at 10 o'clock yesterday morning, in the presence of the Duke of York, the Duke of Kent and the Duke of Gloucester. They all signed the document as witnesses of their brother's act.

The Duke of York went to Fort Belvedere, by car from London last night, for a final dinner with the King before he embarks on his exile. After dinner, the Duke returned to London and, early this morning, visited his mother at Marlborough House.

News Taken

Calmly

Nothing is yet known of the arrangements that will be made for King Edward's future income. The new Civil List, by which it will be governed, will not be drawn up till after Christmas.

THE DUKE OF YORK, who succeeds King Edward on the Throne, photographed late last night when he arrived at 145, Piccadilly, his London home, from Windsor Lodge.

CROWDS CHEER DUKE

Police Have To Clear Way For Car

A GREAT CROWD packing Piccadilly last night, broke into wave upon wave of cheers, when the new King returned to his home there last night.

Motor horns shrieked in salute as thousands of people swarmed round his car.

All traffic in Piccadilly was disorganised. Buses and taxis blocked the roadway and extra police were raced to the spot to control the crowd.

The new King smiled to women who jumped on the running-board and peered in.

ON RAILINGS

At last he was able to step from his car. As he did so, he turned to the crowd and raised his hat several times.

Men and women climbed the railings and every other vantage point to catch a glimpse of him. Scores clambered on the roofs of taxis.

As he went inside the House the crowd sang the National Anthem.

A few minutes after midnight the new King left the house again and drove to Marlborough House to see Queen Mary.

AT PALACE

A crowd of several thousands dislocated traffic outside Buckingham Palace and mounted police rode on the pavements to clear them from the Palace railings.

In vain the police assured the crowd that neither King Edward nor the new King was inside.

A number of young men and women shouted "We want Edward," but others sang the National Anthem.

Shortly before midnight extra police were called from Scotland Yard to deal with a crowd of a few hundred people who had assembled in Whitehall, opposite Downing-street. Police herded them to Trafalgar-square. As they moved off shouts of " We want Edward " mingled with cheers and cries of " God Save the King."

Earlier in the evening a cordon of 26 police was thrown across the Whitehall entrance to Downing-street when Blackshirts tried to demonstrate.

Six people arrested during the demonstration in Whitehall will appear at Bow-street police court this morning.

NO COINS OF KING EDWARD

RUSH TO BUY STAMPS

No King Edward VIII coins will ever be in circulation.

No issue could have been made before a royal proclamation, announcing the date on which the coinage would come into circulation.

Such a proclamation was expected this month. It would have described the design for the King's head and the designs of the reverse sides for the different denominations.

The existing King Edward stamps will be issued until the stocks are exhausted.

Within a quarter of an hour of the abdication announcement were raided yesterday at Southampton new post offices at philatelists, who purchased all King Edward stamps of the higher denominations.

ONE WIRELESS PROGRAMME TO-DAY

The B.B.C. announced late last night that a single programme only would be broadcast throughout to-day from all transmitters.

All transmissions will cease after King Edward has spoken.

(See Page 17.)

The Duke and Duchess of Windsor on their ill-judged visit to fascist Germany in 1937. The visit fuelled untimely rumours about the depth of the Duke's pro-German feelings.

just as he had been 'Dickie's', also declined the invitation drew the couple's lifelong ire.

The deepest cut came at the time of the wedding itself, on 3 June 1937, when the Duke received from Monckton a communication from the King, saying that although he could style himself 'His Royal Highness' neither his wife nor any descendants of theirs would be permitted to do so. The fear that the marriage might not last, or that any future children of theirs might seem to those ignorant of the Constitution to have a better claim to the throne than Princess Elizabeth, added to the loathing felt for an adventuress whom no one trusted, combined to create an act almost calculated to incite life-long bitterness. All British precedent and law was against the act of separating the style and status of the husband from the wife; indeed it was precisely because it had been impossible to do this that the Duke had abdicated in the first place.

What had been genuinely tragic about the former King's life swiftly degenerated into the farcical. Suddenly he had nothing, or at least nothing worthwhile, to do. In October 1937, keen to have the Duchess accorded full state honours by a Great Power, the couple made a fantastically ill-judged visit to Germany, ostensibly 'for the purpose of studying housing and working conditions'. The authorities in London were furious. 'A bombshell and a bad one,' the King wrote to Monckton, who could nevertheless do nothing to prevent the trip taking place.

The Nazi high command, which believed that the King had been forced to abdicate for his pro-German views, laid out the red carpet, and the delighted couple took tea with Hitler himself at Berchtesgaden. This inevitably fuelled rumours about his willingness to consider returning to the British throne under German dictation in the event of a German victory over Britain, doubts which persist to this day. Whether he would, doubtless encouraged by his genuinely pro-German wife, have ever really made such a Faustian compact must of course be a matter for speculation rather than history.

September 1939 found the couple in their French Riviera home La Cröe in Cap d'Antibes. The destroyer HMS *Kelly*, commanded by Mountbatten, brought him back to Portsmouth, where there were no family or state representatives to meet him at the quayside. Instead, after a brief and cool interview with his brother at Buckingham Palace, to which the Duchess was pointedly not invited, it was arranged that he should be attached, with the rank of Major-General, to the British Military Mission in France. Further limitations and humiliating restrictions were regularly placed upon him once out there, despite his best intentions to help the war effort. When France fell in May and June 1940 he behaved characteristically selfishly in leaving his friend, long-time equerry and best man Major Edward 'Fruity' Metcalfe badly in the lurch and escaping first to La Cröe and then to neutral Madrid and Portugal.

A daring German plot was hatched to kidnap the Duke and take him first to Franco's Spain and eventually to Germany, presumably for use as a future puppet king of an occupied Britain. The British government, now led by his old friend and former supporter Winston Churchill, was demanding his return to Britain, and the prime minister even threatened

The Duke and Duchess of Windsor photographed during a visit to Venice in the early 1960s.

a formal court-martial if he continued to refuse. Meanwhile the Duke was tactlessly dining with German agents and predicting military disaster for Britain, whilst attempting to make conditions to the British Government for his return.

These began with demands that he be allowed to serve in a significant capacity, and that his wife should have equal ranking to royal duchesses, but eventually wound down to a request that the court circular be allowed to state that the King and Queen had invited the Duke

Opposite: The Duke of Windsor with his now wife, the former Wallis Simpson'. The mood suggested by this photograph contrasts with the bitterness the 'royal' couple felt at their treatment by the establishment.

Edward spent the last twenty-seven years of his life in exile in France. He is pictured here attending a dinner party in Paris during 1960. The Duke and the Duchess were unable to come to terms with the fact that they were not, in any real sense, a part of the royal family. Edward was still referring to himself as 'King' in the months before his death in 1972.

and Duchess to Buckingham Palace, if only for a quarter of an hour. As his obituary in *The Times* was to put it: 'Although his pride was touched, England's "darkest hour" was an unfortunate moment at which to make an issue of this matter.' The Duke also requested the German authorities to put a guard on his houses in Paris and the Riviera for the duration of the war, which they obligingly did.

With the pressure mounting on him, and the royal family entirely refusing to grant even the shortest formal interview to the couple in order to prove they were not in disgrace, the Duke reluctantly accepted the Governorship of the Bahamas, one of the Empire's least significant colonies, and sailed from Lisbon on 1 August 1940, to general relief in Whitehall. When they arrived they found the authorities had been specifically instructed by the Palace to let it be known that no one should on any account curtsey to the Duchess. For the rest of the war they stayed in the Bahamas, with occasional shopping trips to America, but in general carrying out his Abdication speech promise to serve George VI, albeit in a relatively menial capacity. He did the job well, but was not accorded the customary gubernatorial interview with the King when he retired in 1945.

Returning to France, where the City of Paris had generously provided him with a beautiful house in the Bois de Boulogne, and the French government had even more generously exempted him altogether from income tax, he lived out the next twenty-seven years in an unrewarding round of golf, gardening, dinner parties, gardening and more golf. Ghost writers helped him produce occasional best-selling books, *A King's Story*, which unfairly blamed everything on his father, in 1951, *The Crown and the People*, a saccharine history of the monarchy from Edward VII's coronation to Queen Elizabeth II's in 1953 and *Family Album* in 1960.

The royalties from these books, his original but reduced stipend from his late brother, and some large and totally illegal currency transactions managed to keep the couple afloat financially. The Duchess's glamorous entertaining made invitations to the house in the Bois de Boulogne sought after in Parisian society, although Prince Charles's diary recollections from a visit made in 1971, eight months before the Duke's death from lung cancer on 28 May 1972, show how much of their lives were led in a penumbra of make-believe: 'I found footmen and pages wearing identical scarlet and black uniforms to the ones ours wear at home. It was rather pathetic seeing that. The eye then wandered to a table in the hall on which lay a red box with "The King" on it ... While we were talking the Duchess kept flitting to and fro like a strange bat ... The whole thing seemed so tragic – the existence, the people and the atmosphere – that I was relieved to escape it after 45 minutes and drive round Paris by night.'

GEORGE VI *r.* 1936-52

GEORGE VI'S REIGN WILL GO DOWN IN history', wrote a waspish Evelyn Waugh to a friend, 'as the most disastrous my country has known since Matilda and Stephen'. As his time on the throne spanned the Nazi annexation of Austria, the Munich crisis, the Second World War, Stalin's domination of Eastern Europe, the independence of India, post-war Austerity and the end of Britain's Great Power status, Waugh might well have been right, but the blame certainly cannot be laid at the door of the intensely well-meaning King.

He exhibited many of the qualities of his father, and indeed his father's reign stood as the model on which George VI himself sought to act. Both ex-naval second sons not expected to succeed to the throne, even their handwriting was similar. They both took Britain through a world war soon after their accessions and, fortified by strong wives and simple religious faith, both eventually won the admiration and even love of the people. But where George V had presided over the first shock to the imperial system, his son had to face the start of its complete unravelling, whilst still fervently believing in its capacity to do good.

Born at York Cottage on the Sandringham estate on 14 December 1895 – the anniversary of the death of the Prince Consort – the second son of the Duke and Duchess of York (later King George V and Queen Mary) was unsurprisingly christened Prince Albert Frederick Arthur George. A shy, lachrymose child, the young Prince endured considerable ill-health in boyhood, contracting gastritis as a result of his nurse's negligence and walking with his legs in splints in order to overcome incipient knock-knees. He grew up in the shade of his loving but authoritative father and also of his elder brother David (the future King

Edward VIII), who seemed to have all the attributes in terms of charm, looks, confidence, sporting ability and popularity which 'Bertie', as the family nicknamed him, lacked. It is hardly surprising therefore that aged eight he developed a profound stammer.

Nor was Prince Albert bright; he entered Osborne Naval College at thirteen, but in the exams he came sixty-eighth out of sixty-eight entrants. This might have been the fault of his tutor, but at Dartmouth only a little later he only managed sixty-first out of sixty-seven. Nevertheless in 1913 he joined the fleet as a midshipman, where he developed further gastritis, complicated by seasickness. It is a great tribute to the bravery of this delicate sub-lieutenant that in May 1916,

The royal family celebrating the coronation of George VI, who had grown up in the shadow if his brother, the future Edward VIII, in 1937.

George VI, then Prince Albert, with a group of cadets on board the *Chippawa* at Niagara in June 1913. He later saw active service at the battle of Jutland in May 1916.

at that most terrible of naval engagements the battle of Jutland, he left his sickbed to fight in the gun turret of HMS *Collingwood*.

The next year he had to undergo an operation on an hitherto-undiagnosed duodenal ulcer. He eventually left the navy and, joining the Royal Naval Air Service, qualified as a pilot. In 1919 he went up to Trinity College, Cambridge, with his friend and cousin Lord Louis Mountbatten. As a second son he had not been closely schooled in constitutional history, but fortunately had an opportunity there to read a little about the role that unbeknownst to him would one day be forced upon him. But it was still chiefly in the field of practical jokes, jolly japes and high-spirited follies, understandable in one who had come through the Great War and who had also suffered ill-health, that the Prince excelled.

A serious side began to emerge with his interest in the welfare of the industrial workforce, which his father always feared might one day become republican. Prince Albert set up the Industrial Welfare Society, under whose auspices he visited factories and workshops, always insisting on having no red carpets or over-formality as he wanted to see the true employment situation for himself, rather than the managements' image of what was happening in the British workplace. In 1921, the year after being created Duke of York, he also inaugurated the Duke of York's camps where in an attempt to break down class barriers, public schoolboys were encouraged to spend camping and hiking weekends with inner city children of the same age. Whilst it is easy to satirise these happy campfire encounters, all sitting crosslegged singing 'Under the Spreading Chestnut Tree', they were, like the Duke himself, well intentioned, idealistic and worthy.

It was in his marriage to Lady Elizabeth Bowes-Lyon, solemnised at their wedding in Westminster Abbey on 26 April 1923, that the Duke of York made the soundest decision of his life. Marriage to a commoner

The future George VI serving tea to wounded servicemen at Buckingham Palace during the First World War.

Lady Elizabeth Bowes-Lyon commences her journey to Westminster Abbey on 26 April 1923 to marry Prince Albert, now the Duke of York. His marriage to a 'commoner' was considered a modernising gesture.

was considered a modernising gesture politically, although one could hardly have found a less common commoner than the daughter of the fourteenth Earl of Strathmore. The King and Queen quickly appreciated the Duchess's gift of being able to place their son at his ease, and develop in him a self-confidence which even began to help him master his stutter. At every future crisis of his life, the Duke had beside him a strong-willed, loving and self-confident wife who also became part business-manager, part private secretary, part public relations adviser.

Living at 145 Piccadilly and Royal Lodge in Windsor Great Park, the couple, who were joined in 1926 by Princess Elizabeth (now Queen Elizabeth II) and in 1930 by Princess Margaret Rose, passed a blissful domestic life. In 1926 the Duke visited the celebrated Australian speech therapist Lionel Logue and embarked on an intensive course which helped control but never entirely eradicate his stammer. There were occasional state visits, to East Africa and the Sudan in 1924 and to New Zealand and Australia in 1927, but otherwise time passed quietly for the royal couple.

By the time of his father's death in January 1936, the Duke of York had heard rumours about his elder brother's love life, but little could prepare him for the conversation the King held with him on 17 November 1936, when he made it clear that he intended to marry Mrs Simpson even if it meant forsaking his throne in order to do so. After a series of meetings and further conversations, both with the King and with Stanley Baldwin the prime minister, Cosmo Lang the Archbishop of Canterbury and the King's confidant, lawyer and friend Walter Monckton, it became clear that nothing could be done to change his brother's mind. He wrote in his diary of 'the awful and ghastly suspense' and when he saw his mother Queen Mary on the evening of 9 December 1936, the night before the Abdication, he 'broke down and sobbed like a child'.

The Duke and Duchess of York leave Buckingham Palace for their honeymoon. The Duchess inspired much of the self-confidence that the Duke had previously and conspicuously lacked.

59

Crowds pack into Trafalgar Square to see the coronation procession of George VI pass through Admiralty Arch and into Whitehall (right). Any vantage point was seized by intrepid sightseers, such as these two men in Piccadilly Circus (below).

The next day he stood witness, along with his other brothers, to the Instrument of Abdication, which was signed at Fort Belvedere on 10 December. The day after that he became King, once Parliament had approved the Instrument and the Royal Assent had been given. His Duchess, the new Queen Elizabeth, a constant rock for him throughout the crisis, was angry and hurt at what she and Queen Mary perceived as the King's dereliction of duty. She was angry too at her beloved but far from robust husband having greatness thrust upon him in this precipitate manner, but was also ready to take on the task. She always blamed her husband's relatively early death from lung cancer not on his huge cigarette consumption, but on the strains imposed upon him by Edward VIII's decision.

The swift and ruthless way in which the Duke and Duchess of Windsor were cut out of British official life was probably more due to Queen Elizabeth's innate political understanding of how they could still harm her husband's position, rather than from any sense of personal spite. How

much the King, who hated personal confrontations, was pressed into action by his Queen we shall probably never exactly know. But the King informed Walter Monckton that he no longer wanted to accept his brother's telephone calls, did nothing to influence the government's seemingly harsh decision to deny the Duchess of Windsor the title of Her Royal Highness and, most poignant of all, he refused to attend his brother's wedding in 1937. When after the outbreak of war the Duke of Windsor returned briefly to London, no attempt was made to mend fences, and the Duchess was pointedly not invited to the short interview

The coronation of George VI at Westminster Abbey on 12 May 1937. The ceremony was held on the same day that had been arranged for Edward VIII's coronation, and George naturally had a 'sinking feeling inside' and could not eat breakfast.

the Duke had with the King at Buckingham Palace. The golden boy of his generation was not about to be allowed to overshadow his still-stammering younger brother.

'I could eat no breakfast,' wrote the King in his diary of the morning of his coronation on 12 May 1937, 'and had a sinking feeling inside.' The ceremony was scheduled to take place on the same day as it had originally been arranged for Edward VIII. Apart from a bishop who stood on the King's robe as he attempted to stand up – 'I had to tell him to get off it pretty sharply as I nearly fell down' – the most traditionally accident-prone of all royal pageants went off successfully.

For his title the King chose to adopt his father's name, and became George VI. It had a welcome feel of continuity to it, which the more Germanic Albert would not have done. Moreover it emphasised the way in which the British establishment intended to present the eleven-month reign of Edward VIII as merely a small unfortunate tear in the silken red carpet of monarchy.

Like many other well-meaning and somewhat naive people, especially those who had fought in the Great War, he simply could not believe that the Nazi leaders could be so evil as to contemplate another war. It was a defect in him as King, but one arising from his essential goodness of heart. It is fortunate that his enthusiastic efforts in support of the National Government's appeasement policy – they even had to restrain him from sending messages to Mussolini and Hitler, which would undoubtedly have been misinterpreted in Rome and Berlin – were easily contained.

More usefully to the government he and the Queen were sent on two important visits abroad, to France in June 1938 and to America and Canada in May and June 1939. These helped cement friendships which within months were to be tested to the utmost. An IRA plot to assassinate the King when in America was also foiled by J. Edgar Hoover's FBI. At President Roosevelt's home in Hyde Park, F. D. R. adopted an avuncular approach to the King, with whom he talked international politics until 1.30 a.m., before patting him on the knee and saying 'Time for bed, young man'. At forty-four, the King was hardly that, but he noted his appreciation of the President's friendliness, asking, 'Why don't my ministers treat me as the President did tonight?'

It was after Chamberlain returned from Munich that the King – whose constitutional duty it was not to show any political favouritism whatever – made a serious political error. By inviting Mr and Mrs Neville

Opposite: George VI, who reluctantly took on the responsibilities of kingship after his brother's abdication, pictured with one of the royal corgis.

Chamberlain on to the balcony of Buckingham Palace under huge spot-lights to wave to the crowds cheering in the rain, he gave an unmistakable sign of royal approval to the Munich Agreement.

If Chamberlain had called a snap general election, as he was being urged to do by some of his closest advisers, this public identification of royal support of the appeasement policy would have greatly helped the National Government against the Labour and Liberal parties. The distinguished political commentator John Grigg has described the King's action as 'the most unconstitutional act by a British Sovereign in the present century. Whatever the rights or wrongs of the Munich Agreement, the relevant point is that it was denounced by the Official Opposition and was to be the subject of debate in Parliament.'

Although it might be easy to see why the King and Queen wished to join with most of the rest of the nation in applauding Munich, part of the reason for having a monarchy is that an impartial power can look calmly and rationally at events in the light of precedent, and not fall for the passing enthusiasms of a fleeting hour. The dismemberment of Czechoslovakia only six months later in March 1939 showed the King's euphoric action for the hubristic mistake it was. No commoner had ever before been invited on to the balcony at Buckingham Palace and anyhow, a great war had not been won, merely a small country let down.

Once the Second World War broke out in September 1939, the King and Queen, once again using George V and Queen Mary as their template, threw themselves into the business of maintaining national morale. They worked tirelessly from 1939 to 1945 in keeping it as high as possible, and it is chiefly for those efforts that they will always be remembered. They had the inestimable advantage over their Great War counterparts of being able to use radio, and, masking his loathing of public speaking, the King made a series of moving broadcasts, with millions of listeners sympathetically willing him not to stutter. His most famous broadcast came at Christmas in 1939, when he made a great effect quoting a little-known poet who had written:

Opposite: Field Marshal Montgomery and George VI in conversation during the Second World War. During the Great War George had served in both the Navy and the Air Force.

I said to the man who stood at the Gate of the Year,
'Give me a light that I may tread safely into the unknown.'
And he replied: 'Go out into the darkness,
And put your hand into the Hand of God.
That shall be better than light, and safer than a known way.'
May that Almighty Hand guide and uphold us all.

The royal couple talk to occupants of London's underground shelters during the Blitz. Their own home, Buckingham Palace, was badly damaged in a daylight raid when two bombs fell on the quadrangle thirty yards from the King.

In May 1940, despite personally preferring the Foreign Secretary and former appeaser Lord Halifax, the King was forced to send for Winston Churchill as prime minister, after Chamberlain was humiliated in the Commons after a debate on the conduct of the campaign in Norway. As one of the only politicians of note who had publicly supported Edward VIII during the Abdication Crisis, Churchill was something of a *bête noire* to the King and Queen. This situation could easily have turned into a serious problem, but both men were too responsible to allow the past to cause difficulties during the country's perilous present. Indeed in the very interview at which the King offered Churchill the premiership he made a bantering joke. As Churchill later recalled: 'His Majesty received me most graciously and bade me sit down. He looked at me searchingly and quizzically for some moments, and then said, "I suppose you don't know why I have sent for you?"

Adopting this mood, I replied, "Sir, I simply couldn't imagine why." He laughed and said, "I want to ask you to form a government." I said I would certainly do so.'

After a few minor skirmishes over political appointments and postponed audiences, which Churchill won, the King came round to him, and by New Year's Day 1941 he fully appreciated Churchill's qualities. 'I could not have a better Prime Minister', he wrote in his diary. The relationship developed into mutual admiration and fast friendship, and Churchill ensured that the King was one of the very few people kept fully informed about both the Enigma decrypts of German telegraphs and the creation and deployment of the nuclear bomb.

On 13 September 1940 Buckingham Palace suffered by far the worst of its nine hits of the war when two bombs fell into the quadrangle during an air raid, exploding thirty yards from where the King was talking to Sir Alexander Hardinge, his Private Secretary. 'The whole thing happening in a matter of seconds,' he noted in his diary, 'we all

King George and Queen Elizabeth were determined to share the privations of war with their subjects. This is George VI's ration book.

Winston Churchill joins the King and Queen with Princess Elizabeth and Princess Margaret Rose on the balcony of Buckingham Palace to acknowledge the crowds on VE Day, 8 May 1945.

wondered why we weren't dead. Two great craters had appeared in the courtyard.' It was the occasion on which Queen Elizabeth, with her superb feel for public relations, commented that she was glad it had happened, as now she could 'look the East End in the face'.

It was their regular visits to areas of Britain devastated by bombing that gave the King the idea of instituting the George Cross and George Medal in 1940, for instances of outstanding civilian gallantry. In an inspired move he awarded the medal, which he had personally devised and designed, to the island of Malta, so moved was he by that island's defiance of the Germans, when he visited it in 1943.

The King made few visits abroad during the war, in contrast to his father's constant travelling to the continent during the First World War, as the changing nature of warfare had made it far more dangerous than in the days of relatively static trench positions. In 1943 he visited Field Marshal Montgomery's Eighth Army in North Africa, under the *nom de guerre* General Lyon, and in the following year he visited Field Marshal Alexander's army in Italy. On D-Day plus ten he went to Normandy and toured the beaches, battlefields and field hospitals. As so many of his subjects had, the royal family experienced personal loss, when George, the Duke of Kent, was killed in a mysterious plane crash, of which there were so many in that war. It was not solely out of reasons of geographical centrality or tradition, therefore, but also out of a genuine wish to celebrate the occasion with their sovereign, that the crowds converged on Buckingham Palace to celebrate VE and VJ Days.

With peace in 1945, to the King's great surprise and irritation, came the defeat of Churchill in the general election. The King told Clement

Part of a collection of intimate photographs taken in 1948 to commemorate the silver wedding anniversary of George VI and Queen Elizabeth. Here the King and Queen are pictured in their private apartments in Buckingham Palace.

Attlee that he had heard of his victory on the six o'clock news, and advised his incoming prime minister to swap Hugh Dalton and Ernest Bevin into the posts of Chancellor of the Exchequer and Foreign Secretary respectively. Although this might have been because he wanted as little contact as possible with the Old Etonian Dalton, whose father had been tutor to his father and whom he considered something of a class traitor – and although Attlee later denied the King's advice had been pivotal in the decision anyhow – it was in the best tradition of the Bagehotian constitutional duty of advice, and Bevin proved an excellent Foreign Secretary.

The King, with only the slightest regret, resigned himself to Labour's policy of stripping him of the title King–Emperor, when his cousin Lord Mountbatten oversaw India's partition and independence. He disliked but also could do nothing to halt the policy of nationalisation. 'He is of course a fairly reactionary person', wrote the Labour

The King and Queen's silver wedding anniversary was celebrated the year after their daughter Princess Elizabeth's marriage to Lieutenant Philip Mountbatten, the son of the exiled Prince Adrew of Greece.

MP Hugh Gaitskell after the King had told him he could not under-
stand Aneurin Bevan's concerns over the imposition of National
Health Service charges for teeth and spectacles. Yet if the holder of a
feudal post the rationale of which is founded in the millennial mists of
history cannot prefer stability to change, it is a cruel world. Like his
father, George VI was deeply pessimistic about the likelihood of the
monarchy surviving at all. 'Everything is going nowadays', he said in
1949, on hearing that the Sackville-West family were passing Knole
Park, their ancestral home, to the National Trust: 'Before long, I shall
have to go myself.'

The year 1947 saw both a successful tour of Southern Africa and the
wedding of Princess Elizabeth to Lieutenant Philip Mountbatten, who
was that day created Duke of Edinburgh. Both as a royal cousin – he was
the son of Prince Andrew of Greece who had been exiled in 1922 – and

In the same year as his
silver wedding anniversary,
King George VI succumbed
to arterio-sclerosis, forcing
him to cancel a royal visit.
It was the first of a number
of serious health problems.

14 November 1951 King
George VI and the Queen,
holding Princess Anne,
celebrate the third birthday
of their eldest grandchild
Prince Charles.

as a brave young naval officer, he commended himself to the King and Queen. Showing just the same faith in his daughter and heir which Edward VII had shown his father, the King gave the Princess access to the red boxes and secret diplomatic telegrams. In the autumn of 1948 a bout of arterio-sclerosis forced the King to cancel a visit to New Zealand, and in the following March the King had to have an operation on his left leg when the blood supply to it failed. In September 1951 his entire left lung had to be removed.

The King bore all this stoically; instead it was usually trifling matters that would induce in him temper tantrums which the family called 'gnashes' and which only his wife was able successfully to defuse. His humour was heavy, his manner sometimes finickety over details.

He had a fine memory for other people's errors and was constantly ticking people off for minor infringements of sartorial rules. Yet his solid religious faith and transparent decency, as well as his skill in helping bring his country through the crises of abdication and war, meant that when he died in his sleep at Sandringham in the early hours of 6 February 1952 – after a good day's hare shooting – King George VI was deeply and genuinely mourned as a monarch who, like his father but not his brother, had put duty before everything.

London pays homage to King George VI with a two-minute silence on 15 February 1952.

ELIZABETH II *r.* 1952-

I DECLARE BEFORE YOU ALL that my whole life, whether it be long or short, shall be devoted to your service and the service of our great Imperial family to which we all belong.' Princess Elizabeth's broadcast speech from Cape Town on 21 April 1947, to mark her twenty-first birthday, defines her reign. Like her father and grandfather, duty has been her watchword.

Born by Caesarean section on 21 April 1926 at her maternal grandparents' Mayfair home, 17 Bruton Street, Princess Elizabeth Alexandra Mary was not expected to succeed to the throne for the first ten years of her life. This meant that the early education of the pretty girl known to the family as 'Lilibet' could be undertaken largely by her mother – with help from Queen Mary and a nurse-governess, Marion Crawford – without it becoming an issue of state. The last monarch not to go to school, she thus had a fairly relaxed, comfortable and private upbringing, which helped turn her into a tidy, somewhat methodical young woman. It was not until she was ten years old that the Abdication made her father King, and her heir to the throne.

During the war, she and her younger sister Margaret Rose (born in 1930) lived at Windsor Castle. She was taught constitutional history by Henry (later Sir Henry) Marten, Provost of Eton. When she heard of Neville Chamberlain's resignation over the radio in May 1940 she cried, but the RAF bombing of the German island of Sylt had a happier effect on her; indeed her pleasure at the news prompted her mother to wonder aloud to the Foreign Secretary Lord Halifax, whether the war would not brutalise the finer feelings of children in general. Soon the Princess was able to do her own bit for the war effort when in 1945 she

Opposite: Queen Elizabeth II in 1992. Witness to some of the greatest changes in the kingdom of any British monarch, she symbolizes stability and tradition.

In 1945 Princess Elizabeth contributed to the war effort by joining the Auxiliary Transport Service and becoming a mechanic. She is pictured explaining her work to her mother (then Queen).

joined, at her own insistence, the Auxiliary Transport Service, and somewhat incongruously became a mechanic, learning about what went on under the bonnets of trucks.

Only weeks before the war started, on 23 July 1939, aged only thirteen, the Princess had fallen in love with a handsome young naval cadet. Visiting the Royal Naval College at Dartmouth on the royal yacht *Victoria and Albert* with her parents, Princess Elizabeth met the tall, blond-haired, eighteen-year-old Prince Philip Mountbatten, nephew of her father's cousin Lord Louis Mountbatten.

At the Captain's House at Dartmouth they played together for an afternoon, Philip athletically jumping over the tennis net, which according to Miss Crawford's 1950 book *The Little Princesses*, left the

Opposite: An unusual study of King George VI with his eldest daughter and heir to the throne, Princess Elizabeth, aged eleven. The princesses were adored by the nation and the Commonwealth.

Opposite: Princess Elizabeth with her striking fiancé Lieutenant Mountbatten Royal Navy (born Prince Philip of Greece), on the occasion of their engagement.

little girls most impressed. '"How good he is Crawfie," said Princess Elizabeth, "How high he can jump." She never took her eyes off him the whole time.' When the royal yacht sailed off the next day, the boat he was rowing was the last to turn back. 'Damn young fool!' exclaimed the King, but his daughter had, as she later permitted a biographer of her father to confirm, fallen in love at first sight.

Whether that first meeting, and the subsequent engagement on 10 July 1947 soon after the Princess's twenty-first birthday, had been somewhat stage-managed by Lord Mountbatten is immaterial. For from their spectacular wedding on 20 November 1947, which was both broadcast and televised on the Princess's advice and for which the tight clothing ration restrictions were rightly relaxed, the marriage proved tremendously successful. Prince Philip's resilience, naval brusqueness, and occasional public gaffes are part of the national anthology, and the Queen's regard for him is undimmed.

Created the Duke of Edinburgh on the morning of the wedding service, Prince Philip swiftly adapted to court life. Originally some courtiers, such as the King's Assistant Private Secretary Sir Alan Lascelles, dismissed him as a 'penniless foreign princeling', but he won the admiration of King George VI, not least for having been mentioned in

Shortly after her engagement to Philip Mountbatten, Princess Elizabeth visited Southern Africa with her sister Margaret, both pictured here at the Victoria Falls Hotel in Rhodesia.

despatches in the naval action against the Italian fleet at the battle of Cape Matapan. The son of Prince Andrew of Greece, he nevertheless took British citizenship in 1947, as soon as the extremely volatile political situation in Greece allowed him to do so. The heir to the throne, Prince Charles Philip Arthur George, was born on 14 November 1948, and was followed by Princess Anne in 1950, Prince Andrew in 1960 and in 1964 by Prince Edward.

It was when the Princess and Duke were on the initial leg of a long tour of the Empire, staying at the Treetops Game Reserve in Kenya on 6 February 1952, that they were informed of the death of the King. He had waved them off from the airport only a week earlier, but when they returned it was a bare-headed Winston Churchill who solemnly received them. As the new Queen stepped from the aeroplane dressed in black, she inspired enormous national sympathy, both for her loss and for the fact that she had now to take on so much responsibility aged only twenty-five.

The body of King George VI arrives at Westminster Hall attended by Queen Elizabeth II alongside her grandmother, the wife of the late George V, and mother.

Dressed in mourning for her father, the new Queen leaves the plane that brought her home from Kenya, to be greeted by her prime minister, Winston Churchill.

Opposite: Princess Elizabeth and the Duke of Edinburgh pictured after their wedding, 20 November 1947.

The televised coronation of Queen Elizabeth II in June 1953 was an occasion to lift the spirits of a nation still recovering from the after-effects of war.

The coronation on 2 June 1953 was also televised on the Queen's insistence, and watched by twenty million Britons, and twelve million more heard it on the radio. Richard Dimbleby's splendid broadcast, the news that Edmund Hillary had conquered Everest, the end of rationing and the national rejoicing at the coronation of a beautiful young queen encouraged some enthusiasts in the press to proclaim a 'New Elizabethan Age'. In fact Britain was facing a long period of relative decline, punctuated by crises which in other countries without a monarchy might have produced constitutional upheaval. Instead of the riots, political instability and collapse of the Fourth Republic which took place in France, the British experience of the traumatic process of decolonisation, aided by the Queen's personal belief in the Commonwealth, was smooth.

There were some critics. When in 1955 Princess Margaret was dissuaded from marrying the handsome former RAF hero Group Captain Peter Townsend because he had been divorced – albeit as the innocent party – some voices were raised against the court's stuffiness and old-fashioned views. In 1957 the distinguished historian Lord Altrincham – later Mr John Grigg – wrote in the *National Review* of the Queen that 'she is out of touch with the modern world and her advisers are a tweedy entourage who know nothing of life outside the restricted circle of the establishment'. He got punched in the street for those remarks, which unfortunately probably represent the settled view of most of the British media today.

Princess Margaret and Group Captain Peter Townsend, pictured together during a tour of South Africa. Princess Margaret was dissuaded from marrying a divorcee.

Lord Mountbatten claimed – although Anthony Eden virulently denied it – that the Queen was opposed to the military operation to recapture the Suez Canal in November 1956. If so, and it is by no means impossible, she had very little actual power to alter events, but probably instead exercised her constitutional duties to advise and warn, rather than to encourage. When Eden had to resign the following January she sent for Harold Macmillan, as was her prerogative, rather than R. A. Butler. This decision has been criticised, but ever since the previous November – when Macmillan had greatly out-performed Butler when addressing the Conservative backbench 1922 Committee during the crisis – opinion had been running Macmillan's way, and the Cabinet, which was sounded out by Lord Salisbury, was overwhelmingly for Macmillan.

More controversy was caused when the Queen had to choose a successor to Macmillan himself in October 1963, when the prime minister, who was suffering from prostate trouble, resigned. In again not sending for Butler, but plumping instead for the aristocratic Scottish landowner and personal friend the fourteenth Earl of Home, the Queen has been criticised severely by some historians. It has been alleged that she was almost an ex-officio member of what the Conservative politician Iain Macleod was to denounce as the 'magic circle' of grandees who connived at this appointment, over the head of the more popular and experienced Butler.

In fact it is not the constitutional duty of the sovereign to pick the best man for the task, merely someone who can command a majority in the House of Commons, as Home did. Had Butler refused to serve under Home, this would have been denied him, and Butler would probably have become prime minister. His nerve failed him, but that cannot be laid at the door of the Queen. Historical research has indicated that Home probably did have more support in the party at the time than Butler anyhow. Nevertheless the Queen can only have been relieved when in 1965 the Conservatives adopted rules for the future election of their own leaders.

In 1969, conscious of the 'tweedy' image that Lord Altrincham had publicly criticised, and believing that an exercise in public relations would boost their (already great) popularity, the Queen, advised by Lord Mountbatten, his son-in-law Lord Brabourne and Prince Philip, took a step to 'let daylight in upon magic'. By sanctioning a 'fly-on-the-wall' TV programme, called *Royal Family*, in which cameras were allowed

Opposite: Four months before his twenty-first birthday, Charles, the Queen's eldest son, was invested as Prince of Wales at Caernavon Castle.

into very informal aspects of royal life, the Queen hoped to ease the family relatively painlessly into the modern world. Unrehearsed conversations were filmed between family members, the Queen was recorded making salad at a barbecue and buying bull's-eyes at the Balmoral village shop. It was very tame by modern-day standards of media intrusion, and 68 per cent of the British public watched.

But television tends to trivialise all it touches, and the House of Windsor was ultimately unable to prevent the liberty they had accorded it being turned into licence. 'A family on the throne is an interesting idea,' wrote Walter Bagehot in *The English Constitution* in 1867, 'it brings down the pride of sovereignty to the level of petty life.' Unfortunately for the dignity and standing of the House of Windsor the encouragement of media interest, even in the most controlled and successful way at first, gave an opportunity to a force more dangerous to the institution of monarchy than were the two world wars and the Abdication combined. In the 1980s a number of factors coalesced to make the massive public interest in the minutiae of royal life a perilously negative rather than positive phenomenon.

In 1975 there was a vivid demonstration of the prerogative powers the Queen still possesses when her Governor-General in Australia, Sir John Kerr, dismissed the democratically elected but incompetent Labour government of Gough Whitlam, forcing a general election which was subsequently won by the Liberal Party. Kerr was acting scrupulously within his rights, but had Labour won the election it would doubtless have accelerated the movement for Australia to become a republic.

The braveness shown by George v and George vi still runs in the family. When a lunatic attempted to kidnap Princess Anne in the Mall in 1974 she showed great aplomb, escaping serious injury when her detective placed himself in the path of a bullet intended for her, receiving serious injury and the George Cross as a result. The Queen herself has also had to endure the nocturnal visit of a man named Michael Fagan to her bedroom, as well as a gun being let off at a parade. On both occasions she behaved with great dignity and calm courage.

Princess Margaret had married the photographer Anthony Armstrong-Jones, who was created Earl of Snowdon, in May 1960, but their separation in 1976 (and divorce in 1978) heralded the beginning of a number of royal splits, none of which can be blamed on the Queen, but which taken together have done much to undermine the image of

The Queen, known to have a quick wit, caught on film by Lord Lichfield in a relaxed moment during celebrations for her silver wedding anniversary in 1972.

the family that the *Royal Family* documentary was intended to convey. Inevitably any account of her reign must touch upon the lives of her children, and especially her daughters-in-law.

Nevertheless, the Silver Jubilee of 1977, with its massive outpouring of affection and thanks from the nation for the Queen's tireless dedication to duty, advertised the underlying fact that whoever else might bring the monarchy into controversy, its central figure was entirely above reproach. Astonishingly, considering the many thousands of royal tours and visits that she has under- taken over the past decades, the Queen has never once made a significant gaffe or embarrassing

Queen Elizabeth II enjoys a walkabout with the Lord Mayor of London during her Jubilee celebrations in 1977.

remark. If sometimes she must feel her work is taken for granted, or not appreciated by a nation and media seemingly only interested in her family's Achilles' heels, it is on occasions such as the Silver Jubilee, the Fiftieth Anniversary of VE Day in 1995 and the forthcoming Golden Jubilee in 2002 that she can be reassured.

In 1978 the Queen had to undertake one of the less agreeable sides of her job, when for economic and strategic reasons it became necessary for her to entertain the brutal dictator President Nicolae Ceaucescu of Romania, in London on a state visit, where she invested him with a British honour. The following year Sir Anthony Blunt, the Surveyor of the Queen's Pictures since 1952, was publicly unmasked as a long-standing KGB spy, a fact she had known since he had confessed to MI5 in 1964. Any action taken by her against him would, it was thought, alert the KGB to the fact that he had been 'turned', so she had to endure the presence of a traitor at Buckingham Palace until his retirement in 1972. When the truth came out in 1979 he was summarily stripped of his knighthood.

Nineteen seventy-nine also saw the callous assassination of Lord Mountbatten by the IRA, a horrific reminder of the risks associated with the Queen's position. Prince Charles, who was close to Lord Mountbatten, was particularly affected by the loss. It was Prince Charles's marriage to Lady Diana Spencer in St Paul's Cathedral on 29 July 1981 that put the royal family on a public relations roller-coaster ride, taking them further, in terms of glamour and name-recognition, than ever before in recent times, but also at other times further down in public estimation than at any other point since Regency times. The dangers of having a Princess of Wales who was beautiful and

The funeral procession of Lord Mountbatten, who was assassinated by the IRA in 1979, passes down the Mall. In attendance are, front row, left to right, Prince Charles, the Duke of Edinburgh and David Hicks, Mountbatten's son in law; rear row, left to right, the Duke of Kent, the Duke of Gloucester and Prince Michael of Kent.

The Queen, the Queen Mother and Princess Margaret watch from the balcony of Buckingham Palace as wartime aircraft fly over as part of the VE Day commemorations in 1995.

photogenic only became apparent when her and her husband's fundamental incompatability emerged in the mid-1980s.

And in 1986 Prince Andrew, the Duke of York – who had distinguished himself as a helicopter pilot during the Falklands War four years earlier – married Sarah Ferguson, the daughter of a former Life Guards officer. She turned out to be thoroughly ill-suited to royal life. A former private secretary to the Queen, Lord Charteris, even went so far as publicly to label her 'vulgar, vulgar, vulgar'. It also ended in a long separation and then divorce, as had Princess Anne's 1973 marriage to Captain Mark Phillips.

In the 1980s a number of coincidental developments tended to place the royal family, although never the Queen herself, in the most unforgiving of spotlights. The end of the deferential society, the arrival of the highly intrusive telephoto camera lens, the acrimonious collapse of the Wales's marriage, the rise of cruel, mocking television satire, and the realisation amongst newspaper editors that 'knocking copy' about the royal family would not engender libel writs but could instead vastly increase circulation, all led to an over-familiarity which soon bred contempt, at least of the younger family members.

Of many low points in that decade, the 1987 television programme, *It's a Royal Knockout*, in which the younger royals cavorted around in joke costumes, was particularly bereft of dignity. The number of holidays

Following pages: The fire at Windsor Castle lights up the night sky on 20 November 1992. The fire lasted for fifteen hours and destroyed over one hundred rooms.

Opposite: Few could have predicted the outcome of the fairytale wedding of Lady Diana Spencer and Prince Charles at St Paul's Cathedral in 1981.

taken by the younger royals was held against them, as was the construction by the Duke and Duchess of York of an architecturally challenged house near Sunningdale.

For the Queen herself, who symbolized traditional values, the divorces of her only sibling and three of her children were acutely painful on a personal as well as political level. In the year 1992 alone – the fortieth anniversary of her accession – the Prince and Princess of Wales and the Duke and Duchess of York separated, part of Windsor Castle burned to the ground, overhasty assurances by the Major government as to who should pay for its rebuilding unwittingly led to a press campaign which forced the Queen to agree to pay income tax, the 'Squidgy-gate' conversations between the Princess of Wales and James Gilbey were published and photographs appeared in the *Daily Mirror* of the Duchess of York in a compromising pedal position with someone claimed to be her 'financial adviser'. At a speech in the Guildhall on 24 November the Queen said ruefully that 'In the words of one of my more sympathetic correspondents, it has turned out to be an annus horribilis'.

Hitherto the Queen's desire to protect the couple's two young children, Prince William (born 21 June 1982) and Prince Harry (born in 1984), had been paramount, but the disloyalty shown by the Princess of Wales on BBC TV's *Panorama* convinced her that the Princess, who by then had committed more than one publicised adulterous affair – was more dangerous inside the family than out. Prince Charles, who had been highly embarrassed when a tape-recording of a private conversation with his mistress, Mrs Camilla Parker-Bowles, was made public, was not himself blameless, especially as he had also publicly admitted his adultery on television to Jonathan Dimbleby. However, in order to protect their children he had repeatedly refused to allow friends to campaign against his wife.

It is impossible at present to know precisely what role the Queen played in all these events, except that she initiated the vital decision that the Prince and Princess of Wales should divorce. However, as the highly professional chief executive of what her father nicknamed 'the Firm', as well as the person who ultimately held the purse-strings, her role was undoubtedly crucial, even if it generally seems to have been reactive rather than proactive. Hailing from an earlier, pre-Freudian generation, who are not obsessed with their own feelings and reactions, the Queen is uninterested in the modern ideas of self-discovery and psychology. This perhaps made her less receptive than others to the

Following pages: Diana's sons Prince William and Prince Harry, her brother Earl Spencer, and her ex-husband Prince Charles watch the hearse bearing the coffin of Diana, Princess of Wales leaving her funeral on 6 September 1997.

New Age interests of her daughters-in-law. Reserved rather than cold, interested but never fascinated, regal but not unapproachable, authoritative but not bossy, she is representative of an earlier and better age.

In the early hours of 31 August 1997 Diana, Princess of Wales was killed in a car crash in a Parisian underpass. The massive outburst of national mourning was turned by popular newspapers, which were relieved not to have been blamed for the death themselves as it had

The Queen and Prince Philip bid an emotional farewell to the Royal Yacht HMS *Britannia* during the decommissioning ceremony at Portsmouth in 1997.

been initially suggested that paparazzi photographers were at fault, into a campaign against the supposed heartlessness of the royal family. 'Show Us You Care, Ma'am' was a representative front-page headline of a national daily paper during the week between the Princess's death and her vast funeral on 6 September 1997. The almost universal media demand was for the royal family to return to London from Balmoral and mourn 'amongst their people', as though Scotland was in some way not part of the realm.

Edmund Burke once wrote that democracy was 'the most shameless thing in the world', and the way in which two grieving adolescents, being consoled by their family in private, were dragged out into the world's media spotlight to mourn in public for the gratification of the populace, was undoubtedly the most shameless moment of the Queen's reign. But adaptability is the House of Windsor's secret weapon, and they returned to London, made tortured photocalls in front of the mountains of flowers, changed the long-standing protocol in relation to the flying of Buckingham Palace flags, and the Queen even made a television broadcast expressing her personal regret at the death.

The family behaved impeccably at the funeral for the Princess, which was watched on television by in excess of nineteen million people in the United Kingdom alone. Although the Queen shed no public tears, she did bow her head to the passing coffin, although whether in a gesture of respect to Diana or to Death is unknown, and she also left her seat to smooth the Royal Standard covering the catafalque in a touchingly maternal gesture.

Tears were shed when the royal yacht *Britannia* was decommissioned in December 1997, without any replacement being proposed by the incoming Labour government. This new era of non-republican anti-royalism – a backlash fuelled by envy and misunderstanding about the royal finances – was appeased by the Queen when she allowed it to be known that she had no objections to a Bill to allow a female child of the monarch the right to inherit the Crown if born before subsequent male children. The Queen also chairs a Way Ahead Committee, which looks into further areas in which the monarchy can be adapted, and arcane practices ended. 'I must not take the easy way out' was her childhood motto.

Having never given an interview, the Queen retains a mystique denied to other more self-publicising royals. Other than preventing Prince Charles from taking part in a private Vatican Mass, we know little

about her religious views, which seem to be in the mainstream of Church of England tradition, tending neither to the High nor Evangelical traditions. Her full role in grooming Juan Carlos for the Spanish throne, her opposition to the United States invasion of Grenada in 1983, her reported anxiety about the Miners' Strike of 1984–5 and her part in bringing Britain together with the Commonwealth on the issue

The marriage of Prince Edward and Sophie Rhys Jones at St George's chapel, Windsor on 19 June 1999. The Prince was created Earl of Wessex upon his marriage.

On 4 August 1999 the Royal Family assembled to celebrate the 99th birthday of HM the Queen Mother. For the monarchy and the public she offers a personal connection to some of the most monumentous events of the twentieth century.

of South African sanctions in 1986 cannot be known for certain for many years to come, but in each case she acted strictly constitutionally.

What is known for sure is that this five-foot-four ultimate professional, with her great knowledge and love both of horses – she is a keen and highly knowledgeable racehorse owner and breeder – and of dogs, especially her trademark corgis, is the very personification of Britishness. By never attempting to be the queen of people's hearts, she has nevertheless won their love and admiration. In the two months after her Internet website was launched in March 1997 it attracted no less that twelve and a half million 'hits'. Having been served by ten prime ministers, she is by far the most experienced public servant in Britain. Most have found her a useful sounding board for their hopes and ideas, and she has treated them equally. 'The Queen doesn't make fine distinctions between politicians of different parties,' Sir Godfrey Agnew, the former clerk of the Privy Council, told the Labour politician Richard Crossman, 'they all roughly belong to the same social category in her view.' Accusations of her not appreciating Margaret Thatcher are disproved by her appointment of the former prime minister both to the blue riband of the Order of the Garter and to the Order of Merit, both honours being in her personal gift. Her relations with Tony Blair, who became Labour Prime Minister in May 1997, are believed to be good, and the prospects are excellent for the monarchy to be able to make a fresh start in recapturing some of the ground it lost during the 1980s and 1990s. As one of the few institutions to have survived the second millenium intact, the monarchy can look to the third with confidence.

Such confidence can only have been increased by the November 1999 victory of the monarchist cause in Australia, in a national referendum on whether that country should become a republic. The Queen Mother's entry into her centenary year also provided a focus for regarding the Royal Family in its long-term historical light, for she represents a vivid personal connection with both the Second World War and the Commonwealth, having been the last Empress of India. The marriage of the Queen's youngest son, Prince Edward, who was granted the title Earl of Wessex, to Miss Sophie Rhys-Jones at Windsor Castle also gave well wishers an opportunity to celebrate.

It will be at Queen Elizabeth II's Golden Jubilee in February 2002 that the British people and the Commonwealth will come together to celebrate their sovereign's half-century upon the Throne. The last golden jubilee – Queen Victoria's in 1887 – saw a huge national outpouring of sincere thanks to the monarch for her unstinting, lifelong efforts on their behalf, and Queen Elizabeth's will doubtless witness much the same enthusiasm. Indeed, it is expected that the Jubilee celebrations will be even more impressive than London's 'Millennium' celebrations of 31 December 1999, over which her Majesty also presided.

Arthur Balfour once said of Queen Victoria that 'the great power of her character was from the combination of great simplicity and modesty with the dignity required by her position in the world', an estimation which could also be made of the present Queen. If the key to the House of Windsor has been in its dedication to duty, which is true of all its monarchs barring Edward VIII, then Queen Elizabeth II can take her place among her ancestors with justifiable pride. She has faithfully kept the great promise of lifelong service she made on her twenty-first birthday, over half a century ago.

INDEX

PICTURE CREDITS

theartarchive: endpapers
Camera Press: pages 2, 8, 62, 76, 78, 79, 87, 92-93
Topham Picturepoint: pages 15, 20, 67, 82
Popperfoto: pages 16, 17, 25, 28-29, 30, 34 (both), 35, 36, 37, 44, 48, 55, 56,
57, 58, 59, 60 (both), 70, 71, 77, 80, 81 (top), 83, 88, 89, 91, 95, 99, 100
Weidenfeld & Nicolson Archives: pages 18, 19, 21, 22, 27, 47, 69, 72, 73
AKG London: pages 23, 40, 51, 52, 61, 75
The Bridgeman Art Library, London: pages 24, 32-33, 39
Barnaby's Picture Library: pages 26, 65
Hulton Getty: pages 45, 50, 66, 68, 81 (bottom), 85, 90
Tim Graham: pages 96-97

Victoria Mary